CALM
in your pocket

ANNA BARNES

CALM IN YOUR POCKET

This edition copyright © Summersdale Publishers Ltd, 2021
First published in 2016 as *How to Be Calm*

Design by Luci Ward

An Hachette UK Company
www.hachette.co.uk

Vie Books, an imprint of Summersdale Publishers Ltd
Part of Octopus Publishing Group Limited
Carmelite House
50 Victoria Embankment
LONDON
EC4Y 0DZ
UK

www.summersdale.com

Printed and bound in China

ISBN: 978-1-78783-660-0

Substantial discounts on bulk quantities of Summersdale books are available to corporations, professional associations and other organizations. For details contact general enquiries: telephone: +44 (0) 1243 771107 or email: enquiries@summersdale.com.

Contents

INTRODUCTION

In a busy and hectic world, we could all benefit from slowing down and creating some peace, space and calm for ourselves. Truly reaching a state of calm might seem unattainable, but with practice it is possible and the impact it can have on your life is immeasurable. A certain amount of pressure can be good for us. It can drive us to take action and feel more energized. If left unchecked, however, pressure can escalate and affect every part of our life, from our diet, to our social life, and how well we sleep at night. Whether you encounter stress at work or at home, the easy-to-follow tips in this book will help you to free your mind of worries and handle the strains of life with greater ease. There is no quick fix, but these tips will start you on the path to a new, calmer outlook.

Techniques for Being Calm

You've made a good start in your search for calm by simply deciding to read about the topic. Within this book you'll find tips that will help you to allay your anxieties, along with simple techniques to relax your body and mind.

IDENTIFY
&CONTROL
THE THINGS THAT
MAKE YOU FRET

Over the course of two weeks,
write down all the things that
make you feel anxious or
stressed, be they places, people
or situations. Rate these stresses
on a scale from one to ten, with
one being only slightly stressful
and ten being the most stressful.
Once you have identified your
high-stress triggers you can
take steps to eliminate them;
for example, if getting the bus
to work is a high-stress situation
for you, try cycling or walking
(which gives you the added
benefit of extra exercise).

slow down

One of the first things to do
in order to build inner calm
is to simply slow down. Many
of us are living our lives at an
ever-faster pace, and trying
to balance a whole range of
commitments from work to family
to relationships. This can leave
us feeling restless and frustrated
when we are forced to stop, for
instance when we have to queue.
Combat this by taking those
moments when your bus is late,
or when you are stuck in traffic, to
do something relaxing like deep
breathing or listening to music.

You're only
here for a short visit.
Don't hurry,
don't worry.
And be sure to
smell the flowers
along the way.

Walter Hagen

LISTEN TO THE WISDOM OF YOUR HEART.

BE
OPEN
TO
POSSIBILITIES.

green

Enjoy what the great outdoors has to offer
by spending more time in your garden, local
park or woods. Being in natural surroundings
can bring a real sense of tranquillity. Going
for a walk along the beach, through the
fields or even just in your garden can
improve your mood, ease muscle tension
and lower blood pressure. Feeling close
to nature can give you the boost you
need to keep calm in stressful situations.

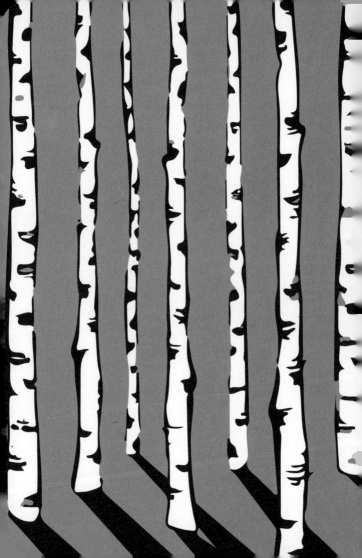

THERE IS A
SERENE AND
SETTLED
MAJESTY TO
WOODLAND
SCENERY THAT
ENTERS INTO
THE SOUL AND
DELIGHTS AND
ELEVATES IT,
AND FILLS IT
WITH NOBLE
INCLINATIONS.

Washington Irving

ENJOY A TREAT A DAY

If you're feeling low, tense or anxious, try doing something nice, however small, each day to lift your spirits. Whether it's putting fresh sheets on the bed, making time to watch your favourite film or TV programme, disappearing under a blanket to read a book, cooking a nice meal or seeing a friend, having something to look forward to throughout the day will help you through and raise your positivity levels. Look at your diary regularly and make sure you have enough going on each week to keep you occupied and happy. And you don't have to spend money to have fun: on a sunny evening go for a walk in the local park; when it's cold, head to a friend's house or investigate the free events in your local area.

The most important thing is to enjoy your life –

TO BE HAPPY

– it's all that matters.

Audrey Hepburn

MAKE A TO-DO LIST

Whether at work or at home, if you
have lists of tasks going round in your
head, this can cause stress and worry.
The simple act of writing a to-do list and
crossing each item off as it is done is very
cathartic, and adds structure to your day-
to-day life, helping you to feel organized
and calm, and giving your brain licence
to switch off when it comes to bedtime.
Remember, you don't have to cross off
every item; just making the list is progress.

Set peace of mind as your highest goal, and organize your life around it.

Brian Tracy

BE PREPARED

If an upcoming event or situation makes you feel tense or uneasy, do your best to prepare for it. This might sound like common sense, but when feeling anxious we sometimes forget to approach things logically. If you have to take a test or an exam, draw up a revision timetable in advance so you can cover all the ground required. If you're worried about giving a presentation at work, spend plenty of time preparing and perhaps ask a colleague to present with you. If you're a nervous driver and the thought of having to use the car scares you, try a driving refresher course. Being prepared for a situation will help you to relax.

The time to relax is when you don't have time for it.

Sydney J. Harris

INVEST IN
SOME "ME" TIME

We often lead very busy lives and
spend our time rushing between
one task and the next both in the
workplace and at home. This constant
high-speed, high-pressure living can
lead to high stress levels. Simply taking
a little time out for yourself every
so often can help you to recharge
your batteries, and can also help you
to concentrate better and feel more
positive. At work, taking a walk in
the fresh air during your lunch break
can help you feel grounded. At home,
taking the time to call a friend or read
a chapter of a book between tasks
will help you to feel more relaxed.

Let your worries drift away like clouds.

Get out in the sunshine

We might be prone to drizzly, grey days in the UK, but when the sun does come out it's important to take advantage of it. Our bodies create most of our vitamin D from direct sunlight and this in turn helps our brains to produce serotonin, the "happy hormone". Fewer hours of sunlight in the winter months can lead us to feel sleepier than usual, as when it is dark our brains produce melatonin, the "sleep hormone", which may make us feel drowsier than we normally do. Evidence suggests that short, daily periods of direct sunlight – just ten to 15 minutes – can provide the vitamin D we need to see us through; after this you should apply sun cream to avoid sun damage.

Be
HAPPY
for
this
moment.

This moment is your LIFE.

Omar Khayyám

Positive Change

If you're feeling stuck in a rut, why not try something new? Get involved in a new hobby or activity. Whether it's joining a gym, signing up to a yoga, Pilates or martial arts course, learning another language or the basics of photography at the local college, or knitting an enormous blanket, it could be a good idea to have a project to get your teeth into, to give you focus and take your mind off your problems. Evening classes and courses are also a good way to meet new people – and remember, everyone is in the same boat, so try to relax and enjoy it.

Never
rush. Do
everything
quietly and
calmly.

Let it out

If things do get on top of you, don't forget that sometimes you might just need to close a door on everything and have a good cry. Tears are the body's way of releasing stress hormones or toxins. Allowing your emotions to surface can leave you feeling somewhat relieved and ready to face the world again.

We must let go of the life
we have planned, so as to accept
the one that is waiting for us.

Joseph Campbell

TRY A SPA DAY

A real treat to send you to new heights of relaxation is to book a spa day or weekend, where there is little to do but swim, sit in a sauna or hot tub, and enjoy blissful treatments, such as an aromatherapy massage or a facial. This needn't be expensive – there are plenty of websites offering discounted spa experiences, and it's likely you'll be able to find one not too far away. Keep an eye on www.groupon.com, www.livingsocial.com, www.lastminute.com and www.spabreaks.com for special offers, and arrange to get away from it all for a day or two. If you're on a budget, invite your friends round for a spa day at home and take it in turns to give each other mini pamper treatments.

Gratitude
brings more
things to
be grateful
for.

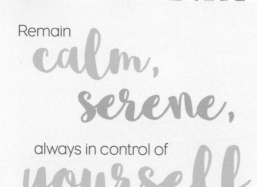

Remain **calm, serene,** always in control of **yourself.** You will then find out how easy it is to **get along.**

Paramahansa Yogananda

ACCEPT YOURSELF
AS YOU ARE.

Calm
in the
Home

Your home should
be a place of refuge;
somewhere you feel happy
and comfortable. If it
has become a source of
stress, the following tips
will help you to turn your
home back into a place
of rest and renewal.

AVOID TOO MUCH TV TIME

Amazingly, the average person watches around four hours of television a day. When you consider how busy our lives have become, it is no wonder we find little time to do anything else if we come home from work, sit in front of the television for four hours and then go to bed. This can add to the feeling of not having enough time and can lead to you feeling overwhelmed. While television can be interesting and informative, watching too much of it can eat into the time you might spend talking to your loved ones or taking part in a hobby. Rather than just turning the television on automatically in the evening, plan what you want to watch and turn the TV off after it has finished.

Televisions are not the only screen we should avoid too much contact with if we want more peace and tranquillity. With the rise in use of technology, many of us sit at a screen for eight hours while at work, only to check our personal emails and social media accounts on our laptop or tablet, and then do additional work, play games or watch catch-up TV on our home computers. All in all, we can end up spending ten or more hours a day looking at a computer screen, which causes eye strain and muscle strain in the neck. This can lead to tension headaches – a major stress factor.

Reduce your contact time with computer screens by making sure you take regular breaks at work, and try to spend time at home away from the computer as much as possible. Making time for conversations with your partner or friends or taking up a hobby can help you to get away from a screen. You will feel physically better, and more calm and composed.

CUT DOWN ON YOUR COMPUTER TIME

I will be

calm.

I will be

mistress of

myself.

Jane Austen

Our freedom can be measured by the number of things we can walk away from.

Vernon Howard

DECLUTTER YOUR HOME

A clean home helps us to keep a clear head. Most of us will know the feeling when you want to find something, be it an item of clothing, a book or a kitchen gadget, but our overflowing drawers, wardrobes and shelves stop us in our tracks. Frustrations can build in situations such as this, and cause us to feel bad-tempered and anxious.

Decluttering our homes can help improve calmness on various levels: with your belongings tidily in place you will not waste time getting stressed looking for them, the act of tidying can be very satisfying and the physical energy involved in decluttering produces serotonin – the hormone that balances mood and helps us to feel happier.

ORGANIZE YOUR WARDROBE

Once you have decluttered, it is time to tackle your wardrobe. It can be stressful deciding what to wear to work in the morning, or to that special social event. Knowing where everything is will allow you to choose your outfits more quickly and easily, leaving you feeling calmer and in control.

The amount of space you have and your own preferences will help you to decide how to organize your clothing, but a couple of simple suggestions would be to either divide your wardrobe into work and casual, and then into colours within those groups, or to divide it into clothing types – tops, trousers, dresses, etc. Choose whatever works best for you.

There is no **GREATNESS** where there is not **SIMPLICITY.**

Leo Tolstoy

TACKLE MONEY MATTERS

If your finances are troubling you, the first
thing to do is get organized and create
a spreadsheet detailing all your monthly
outgoings. Then, work out where you
might be able to cut back. Do you have the
best possible energy tariff, for example?
There are several price-comparison
websites that could help you switch to a
more cost-efficient price plan. What about
your mobile phone: are you paying for
"free" minutes that you don't actually use?
It might be time to downgrade or switch
to a pay-as-you-go or SIM-only deal.
How much food do you throw away each
week/month? Make shopping lists and
stick to them, freeze any leftovers to eat
at a later date and use a price-comparison
site such as www.mysupermarket.co.uk
to make sure you're shopping sensibly.

NOTHING CAN BRING YOU

Peace

BUT

Yourself.

Ralph Waldo Emerson

FOCUS ON WHERE YOU'RE *going,*

NOT WHAT YOU'VE LEFT *behind.*

SPEED-CLEAN YOUR WAY TO A CALMER HOME

Trying to keep on top of household chores when you are balancing your commitments to your job, your family and your friends can be rather daunting. If you feel it's time to take on the grime, but are overwhelmed by the size of the job, take the stress out of cleaning by tackling just one or two rooms at a time, rather than the whole job. You don't need to clean everything in the room, just whatever is dusty or dirty, and if you wear an apron with pockets, you can carry your cleaning equipment round with you. Finally, remember that big tasks such as cleaning the windows or the oven don't need to be done as frequently. Spread them out throughout the year to reduce the cleaning you have to do on each occasion.

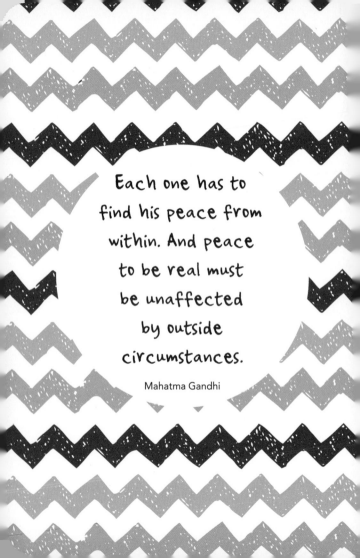

Each one has to
find his peace from
within. And peace
to be real must
be unaffected
by outside
circumstances.

Mahatma Gandhi

SLEEP WELL, FEEL WELL.

Improving your sleep will help you feel better and think more clearly. Sleep is the body's way of recharging itself, both physically and mentally. When you sleep better, life's difficulties and challenges can seem a little less stressful than they otherwise would.

WORK OUT HOW MUCH SLEEP YOU NEED

The optimum amount of sleep for most adults is between seven and nine hours a night, but everyone differs. The best way to figure out how much sleep you need is to listen to your body. Regardless of whether you're meeting the recommended guidelines or not, if you feel rested, you're probably getting enough sleep, and if you constantly feel tired, you're probably not! Work out the ideal number of hours' sleep you need and try to stick to this.

Make your bedroom enticing

Make your bedroom your sanctuary – a place for sleep and sex only. Leave your worries in another room and switch off while you prepare for sleep. One of the best ways to promote restful sleep is to declutter your surroundings. Keep your bedroom tidy, with floors clear, and find a home somewhere else in the house for everything that doesn't naturally belong there. Remove any tablets, phones, laptops and TVs – screen time should be limited before bedtime to prevent your brain "waking up" when it's really time to go to sleep. Read a book or a magazine instead. Opt for soft lighting to give the room a warm glow, and try scented candles or oils to further create a relaxing and pleasant atmosphere. Lavender, chamomile, jasmine and vanilla are all believed to promote restful sleep.

LEARN TO CLEAR YOUR MIND

One of the most common causes of sleep loss is an overburdened mind. We've all experienced it, some more than others. It's important to learn to pack up your worries before you head to bed. You might find that writing down how you're feeling will help to unburden you – perhaps you could write in a diary or make a to-do list for the next day. You might also find that talking to a friend or family member helps to calm you; the aim is to feel as stress-free as possible before your head hits the pillow.

Devise a
bedtime routine

If you find yourself feeling tense at bedtime and not ready for restful sleep, try devising a bedtime routine. If you stick to it, a routine around the time you'd like to go to bed will help to let your body know that it's time to go to sleep and prepare accordingly. Perhaps you could have a bath, followed by a hot drink while you read a book. If possible, choose a herbal drink featuring lavender, chamomile, vanilla, hops or valerian. If this doesn't do the trick, you could try something a little stronger, such as valerian root tablets, which are widely available, or a relaxing pillow spray. Eventually, these regular pre-bedtime activities will act as triggers and tell your body and mind to switch off and go to sleep.

Make your expectations realistic

Many of us lie awake at night worrying that we won't get the recommended eight hours of sleep that we need to function well. However, the "worry" part of this scenario is what has the biggest negative effect. Studies have shown that most people will have no problem functioning with six or seven hours' sleep, and furthermore, that if you have lost sleep, you only need to catch up on about a third of the lost time to get back to normal. For example, if you went to bed an hour and a half late one night of the week, a thirty-minute lie-in at the weekend would do the trick. Changing our perceptions of the time we need to sleep can help us to feel more secure, and therefore help us sleep more easily, with a better quality of sleep.

Remember when life's path is steep

to keep your
mind even.

Horace

the the the the the the th
the the the the the the th
the the the the the the th
the the the the the the th
the the the the the the th
the the the the the the th
the the the the the the th
the the the the the the th
the the the the the the th
the the the the the the th
the the the the the the th
the the the the the the th
the the the the the the th
the the the the ...ZZZ

CLEAR YOUR MIND

Sometimes the mind refuses to be quiet. In these cases, repeating a word which doesn't mean anything can help clear your mind of thoughts and, helpfully, induce boredom. One recommendation is to use the word "the", as this is short and means nothing on its own, though you can choose any word you think will work for you. Try repeating the word in your head every two seconds for five to ten minutes and let your mind be soothed into sleep.

Let peace
be your
middle
name.

Ntathu Allen

Let your worries float away

This visualization will help when seemingly insurmountable worries start circling round in your mind at night. If your mind is racing, looking for a solution it can't find, tell yourself, "I can't do anything practical to help this today – I can think about it in the morning." As you give your mind this message, see your worry trapped inside a colourful balloon, floating up and away, out of reach and out of mind.

MAGNESIUM: NATURE'S TRANQUILIZER

Magnesium is an essential nutrient that helps the body to function well, particularly when it comes to sleep. A lack of this mineral has been linked to early waking. Magnesium helps you to relax, calming the mind and the body, and can alleviate night cramps. Recommended daily intakes of magnesium are 270 mg for men and 300 mg for women, all of which you can get from a balanced diet. Magnesium-rich foods include dark-green leafy vegetables such as spinach or broccoli, nuts, beans, herbs and oats. Eat plenty and reap the benefits.

try living at a slower pace.

A Sense of Calm at Work

It's likely that you spend more time at work than at home with your family. If your job leads you to have regular bouts of anxiety – perhaps it's a high-pressure position, or you have a particularly demanding boss or colleagues – there are steps you can take to help improve your situation.

Define what is
necessary for you
to do and say

to the rest.

IMPROVE YOUR WORKSPACE

We spend hours at work and yet most of us spend very little time thinking about our workspace. Make your work environment a nicer place to be: add a plant or a photograph to your area and declutter for a sense of calm. Research shows that people work best in natural sunlight but if that's not an option, try natural daylight bulbs or a monitor hood to reduce the glare from overhead lights. It's hard to relax if you feel uncomfortable, so make sure your keyboard and mouse are set up correctly and invest in ergonomic seating if possible.

WHEN SOMETHING FEELS HEAVY,

BREAK
IT
DOWN

UNTIL ONE PIECE OF IT IS LIGHT ENOUGH TO HANDLE.

BEGIN THERE.

Bernie S. Siegel

I hope for nothing.

I fear nothing.

I am free.

Nikos Kazantzakis

LEARN TO SAY
NO

We all want to do well in our jobs, but it can be easy to fall into the habit of always accepting work and piling the pressure upon ourselves. The concept of saying "no" to your superior when they ask you to complete a task can be a daunting one, but it is important not to worry that you will lose respect if you refuse. Those in charge understand that sometimes our workload does not permit us to take on additional tasks and responsibilities; they rely on their employees to let them know when and if they are able to do more. Politely declining a task with the explanation that you will not be able to complete it in the time needed will not only show your boss that you are aware of your workload and limits, it will also help alleviate your stress. If you always feel you have to say "yes" then you may be left with too much work, and will have the added pressure of finishing tasks late, of not completing them to the desired quality, or of having to work additional hours to complete them. This is easy to avoid, just keep an awareness of what you need to do, and say "no" if you need to.

Let your soul stand cool and composed

before a million universes

Walt Whitman

STRETCH...

If you have a desk-based or sedentary job, getting up to stretch every couple of hours gives your eyes a break from the computer screen or project at hand. As well as this, it helps to prevent muscular tension, which can lead to headaches, and it is good for circulation. When our muscles are tense we become more emotionally tense, and more inclined to feel stress, so stretch that work tension away.

STOP

a moment,

cease your work,

look around you.

Leo Tolstoy

Focus

on

one

thing

at a

time.

Avoid "catching" stress from your colleagues

One of the biggest barriers to feeling calm at work is so-called "second-hand" stress. When a colleague is feeling stressed you can subconsciously "absorb" their feelings of negativity. To avoid this, if a colleague is talking about work or personal problems, try to say something positive about the subject or offer them some advice. If they carry on, perhaps offer to go and make a hot drink to defuse the situation, or if you cannot walk away, make sure you stay positive and try your best not to adopt your colleague's mindset.

**When you
are content
to be simply
yourself and
don't compare
or compete,
everybody will
respect you.**

Lao Tzu

TAKE A HOLIDAY

Whatever your job, it's vital that you take regular breaks from work and spend time doing what makes you happy. Whether you go on holiday or stay at home, you need time away from your daily work routine to relax and switch off, and just forget about it all for a few days or a week. The "staycation" has become ever more popular, while many people take time off to get things done that they wouldn't usually have time for – such as odd jobs around the house or catching up with friends.

Bring a bit of nature into the office

Surprising as it may seem, research shows that having a plant on your desk can help to lower stress levels and even boost productivity. It is thought that the calming effects of nature, as well as the purifying effects of oxygen-producing foliage, are to thank for this positive reaction. Choose leafy plants rather than flowering ones, as plants rich in foliage will produce more oxygen.

Nature teaches us simplicity
and contentment, because in
its presence we realize we need
very little to be happy.

Mark Coleman

Talk to someone

Are you finding work taxing? You're not alone. More and more people are finding themselves overworked and underpaid, as many businesses struggle to compete and are forced to lay off staff. There's still just as much work to do, but fewer people to do it. If your job is starting to make you feel anxious all the time, even when you're at home, perhaps you should talk to someone. If your line manager or boss is not the approachable sort, how about telling a colleague and see if they're feeling the same way. If you are still concerned, you could talk to someone in the HR department, who should be able to provide support, help and advice. This is your health and well-being after all.

Cultivate peace.
Commit to peace.

Insist on it.

Melody Beattie

Calm the mind

Stress is inevitable in our lives, but how we handle it is a choice. By adopting a positive attitude and being kinder to ourselves, we can remain calm and unruffled in the midst of challenging situations.

Learn problem-solving

Issues can mount up, and thinking about them excessively can make them seem like insurmountable problems. When we mull over a situation, we may think that we are looking for the best solution, but in fact we can be causing the worries surrounding this problem to grow, just with the action of thinking alone. Instead of thinking over your problems, try taking positive steps to change difficult situations. Even if you are only moving slowly towards the goal of eliminating the issue, just focusing your energy on what you can do now can have a very positive effect on your emotional health.

Negative?
What negative?

We will all experience difficult situations at some point or other in our lives, but it is how we deal with them, and not the situations themselves, that has the most impact on how we feel. A great way to change your mind about problems is to find a positive within the negative. This can be hard at first, especially in situations that can have quite a strong and lasting effect on your life. Even finding a small positive will make a situation easier to deal with. Perhaps you have lost your job, but the positive is that now you can retrain for the career you always wanted. Or perhaps a relationship has ended, but the positive is that you are now free to find someone more suited to you. It is not always easy to do this, but this shift in perspective can be very liberating.

Very little is
needed to make
a **HAPPY LIFE**;
it is all within
YOURSELF,
in your way
of thinking.

Marcus Aurelius

Focusing on the positive eases life's stresses.

Use
affirmations

An affirmation is a positive phrase that you use to help change negative beliefs to positive ones. Affirmations work well when written down and when said out loud. A positive affirmation to help you change your attitude to stressful situations could be,

"I feel calm and centred"

or

"I solve my problems quickly and effectively".

It is important that the affirmation focuses on the positive outcome that you want rather than the negative possibility that you wish to avoid, and that it is written or spoken in the present. You can buy CDs of positive affirmations to listen to before sleep, or download them from the internet, should you prefer.

Instead of wondering when your next vacation is, maybe you should set up a life you don't need to escape from.

Seth Godin

WORRY PRETENDS TO BE
NECESSARY BUT SERVES
NO USEFUL PURPOSE.

Eckhart Tolle

Live every day
as though it
were your first
– with curiosity
and wonder.

Talk about it

One of the best things you can do when trying to understand your disquiet, and where it comes from, is to talk to a friend or family member. Vocalizing your concerns is not only cathartic, but may help you to understand why you feel the way you do; and if you speak to someone who knows you well, they may be able to offer valuable insight into how they perceive your recent behaviour. You're also likely to feel a sense of relief after speaking to someone whom you trust, so give it a go and confide in someone close to you.

After a STORM comes a CALM

Matthew Henry

Step into a future full of new hopes.

Know your goals

Do you know what you want from life? Are you happy in your work? What about your home and personal life? If your current life situation is causing you to feel negative or overwhelmed, it could be time to make some changes. Think about your job, your relationships, your finances and your friendships. What could you change that might make you feel more positive going forward? Set realistic goals that help you to feel inspired to make changes – and choose the goals that are right for you, not to please anyone else. Try writing down your aspirations and, if it suits, create a realistic plan detailing when you hope to have achieved them. If it's a career change that you crave, why not do some research and seek professional career advice? Tell yourself that by this time next year you will be on the path to making a change in that area of your life.

Learn to manage your thoughts

It's important to learn how to switch off – don't let worries follow you around all day. When at work, focus on the task at hand and try not to let your mind wander to other aspects of your life that may be causing you to feel tense. If a stressful work environment is getting you down out of hours, try to leave all negative thoughts about your job in the workplace when you clock out for the day. If you find it difficult to switch off in the evenings, make plans to take your mind off work – see friends, go to the cinema or sign up for that evening class you've always been meaning to take.

HE WHO HAS A

IN LIFE CAN
TOLERATE
ALMOST ANY

Friedrich Nietzsche

Join a support group

Don't feel that you are alone in suffering from low mood or anxiety; the Mental Health Foundation estimates that one in four people in the UK will experience a mental health issue over the course of a year, and claims anxiety and depression are the most common mental health disorders in the country. Mind, the mental health charity, offers help and advice, either over the phone or via its website www.mind.org.uk, and has centres located in major towns and cities offering crisis helplines, supported housing and counselling. Search for support groups in your local area and spend some time with people experiencing similar difficulties – it will be just as beneficial for them as it will be for you.

Contentment is natural wealth,

LUXURY IS ARTIFICIAL POVERTY.

Socrates

Eating for a Quiet Life

Good nutrition is essential for both our physical and mental health. The following tips reveal which foods can help promote your inner serenity.

Balanced Diet

There are foods that are said to be good for the heart, the brain and digestion – and there are foods that increase stress or promote calm. The first thing you should try to do, though, is to get a balanced diet. Eating the right amount of calories for your age, height and sex, and ensuring you get enough protein, fibre and vitamin-rich fruits and vegetables will give you a sound basis for general health and should improve your digestion. Eating a balanced diet puts you in the best shape to fight stress and acts as an excellent starting point for "de-stress" nutrition.

EAT
REGULARLY

When assessing your diet and how
you might be able to change it
to improve your mood, the most
important factor is the regularity
of your meals. It's important to
eat three meals a day at regularly
spaced intervals in order to maintain
blood sugar levels. Breakfast really
is the most important meal of
the day – if you skip this you will
experience a dip in blood sugar
and this can lead to low mood.
If you start to feel hungry and
irritable in between meals, reach
for a healthy snack, such as a
banana or a handful of nuts.

Eat your five a day

The recommended daily intake of fruit and vegetables is at least five portions a day. The fruit and vegetables you need the most are those containing B vitamins and vitamin C – all linked to healthy brain function – as these will help your body to feel calmer and boost your mood. Find B vitamins in green leafy vegetables, beetroot, mushrooms and citrus fruits; and find vitamin C in oranges, red and green peppers, broccoli, strawberries, blackcurrants, Brussels sprouts and potatoes. It's also important to keep up levels of vitamins D and E, which are both found to support better mental function: find vitamin D in oily fish, such as salmon, mackerel and sardines, eggs and fortified breakfast cereals; and find vitamin E in nuts, seeds and fortified cereals.

OUR
ENTIRE LIFE
CONSISTS
ULTIMATELY
IN ACCEPTING
OURSELVES
AS WE ARE.

Jean Anouilh

Focus on
Healthy Fats

Not all fats are bad news. We all need to consume enough healthy fats to keep our brain functioning properly, and research has found that those who diet and cut out all types of fat can suffer from symptoms of anxiety and depression. The worst type of dietary fat is trans fat (or "partially hydrogenated vegetable oil"), which is mainly found in processed food such as baked goods, snacks and fried food.

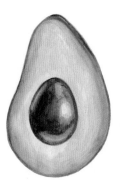

It's best to minimize your consumption of these sorts of foods as trans fats have been linked to coronary heart disease. However, polyunsaturated fats are vital in maintaining a healthy brain, while monounsaturated fats are rich in vitamin E, and both can help to lower cholesterol. The former can be found in walnuts, peanuts, sesame and sunflower seeds, olive oil and oily fish; while the latter can be found in nuts, olives and avocados. Saturated fat (found in certain meats, dairy products and coconut oil) is also thought to play a key role in our health and may be consumed in moderation.

DON'T REACH FOR THE SALT

Being under strain for long periods of time can make us crave salt, as our adrenal glands become exhausted and are unable to make adrenaline and cortisol. This results in a salt imbalance, and it can be very easy to reach for salty foods – especially as many of these foods are also fatty and comforting. Although high salt intake alone does not increase stress levels, the associated health problems such as weight gain and high blood pressure certainly do, so give salt a wide berth. Instead, choose fruit as a snack, and prepare your meals from fresh produce as pre-packaged foods are usually very high in salt.

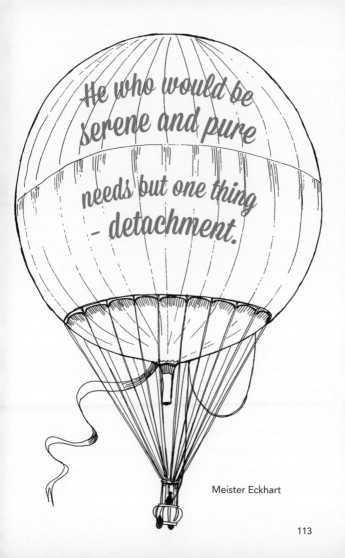

He who would be serene and pure needs but one thing - detachment.

Meister Eckhart

PEP UP WITH PROTEIN

It's important to eat enough protein, particularly when you're going through a difficult time. Protein helps your brain to absorb tryptophan, which is the amino acid needed for the production of serotonin. Tryptophan and protein-rich foods include chicken, lamb, fish, soya beans and many nuts and seeds. Walnuts, flaxseeds, pumpkin and sunflower seeds are a particularly good source of tryptophan; sprinkle them on salads or, if you're not a big fan, use a coffee grinder to reduce them to a fine powder, and add the mixture to soups and stews. You won't even know it's there, but will be reaping the benefits. Tryptophan-rich foods could well help you sleep better and elevate your mood, too.

good food, good mood.

CURB YOUR SWEET TOOTH

When stressed, it can be easy to reach for sweet foods for the quick surge of energy they give, and for the comfort. Part of the reason people do this is that we have an inbuilt reaction to danger, known as "fight or flight". Our reaction has not yet evolved to catch up with our modern lifestyle, and stress is still perceived by our bodies as a reaction to being in danger. When faced with a predator, for example, we would need to stand and fight, or quickly run away, and for both of these, we would need quick-release energy. To give your body the sweet taste it is craving, try eating naturally sweet foods such as carrots, sweet potatoes, berries and coconut rather than sugary sweets or snacks.

BE ACE

High levels of stress hormones in your system can have a negative effect on your health, either by lowering your immune system, making you more prone to coughs, colds and other infections, or by over-stimulating it and provoking autoimmune illnesses and inflammation of the body. A simple way to combat this is to eat plenty of foods rich in the antioxidant vitamins A, C and E. These antioxidants help normalize the body and reduce inflammation, while boosting immunity.

Vitamin A is found in the form of retinol in products such as fish liver oil and egg yolks. Too much retinol can be bad for the health though, so balance this with beta-carotene, found in mainly yellow and orange fruits and vegetables such as carrots, butternut squash and apricots. Vitamin C is found in good amounts in citrus fruits, broccoli, berries and tomatoes, and vitamin E is found in nuts, seeds, avocados, olive oil and wheatgerm. Adding some of these foods to your diet could make you feel healthier and happier.

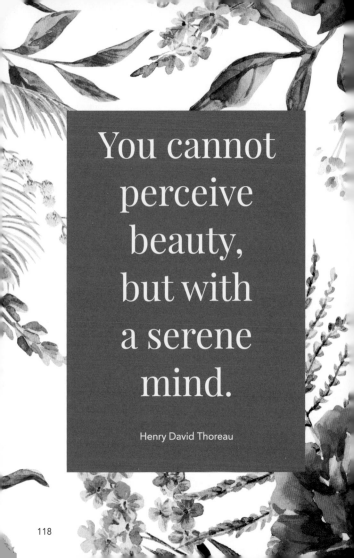

You cannot perceive beauty, but with a serene mind.

Henry David Thoreau

DON'T RACE FOR
THE FINISH LINE;

enjoy

the

journey.

GET A B-VIT BOOST

The B vitamin group is
particularly important for
helping you to calm your nerves.
Among their other functions,
B vitamins are involved in the body's
control of tryptophan, a building block for
serotonin. Too little tryptophan can lead
to a drop of serotonin, which can lead
to low mood, which, in turn, can lead to
very serious psychological problems. The
main vitamins to pay attention to are B1,
B3, B5, B6, B9 and B12, all of which can
be found in a balanced diet, especially in
foods such as spinach, broccoli, asparagus
and liver. If you eat a lot of processed
foods, or are a vegan, you may be
lacking in certain B vitamins, in which
case adding a B-vitamin supplement to
your diet can have an excellent effect.

LEARN TO GET IN
TOUCH WITH THE
SILENCE WITHIN
YOURSELF AND
KNOW THAT
EVERYTHING
IN LIFE HAS
A PURPOSE.

Elizabeth Kübler-Ross

GIVE GREEN TEA A GO

If you're trying to cut down on caffeine, consider replacing some of your daily cups of tea or coffee with green tea. Green tea contains much lower levels of caffeine and the amino acid L-Theanine, which has been found to have calming effects, and many claim it's a good anti-anxiety remedy. If you don't like the taste of straight green tea, why not try one of the many variants on the market? Green teas are available in a multitude of flavours, including strawberry, mandarin, echinacea (good for warding off colds), mint, ginseng (for that all-important pick-me-up you won't be getting from your caffeine fix) and nettle.

Keep
your mind
open and
ready to
accept new
thoughts.

We must not allow the clock and the calendar to blind us to the fact that each moment of life is a miracle and mystery.

H. G. Wells

CUT DOWN ON ALCOHOL

After a hard day at work, many people will reach for a drink to help them relax. Alcohol does have an instantly calming effect, but this is negated by the depressant qualities of alcohol and the feeling of anxiety that can be left behind once the effects wear off. Alcohol can also disturb your sleep, contrary to the popular idea of a "nightcap". Try to cut down your drinking as much as possible, and if you do go for a tipple, opt for a small glass of Chianti, Merlot or Cabernet Sauvignon, as the grape skins used in these wines are rich with the sleep hormone, melatonin. Do make sure it's a small one, though!

A man of calm is like
a shady tree. People who
need shelter come to it.

Toba Beta

MAX YOUR MINERALS

Minerals are essential for a healthy nervous system, so to ensure general physical and mental well-being, you need to consume the correct amounts. Calcium deficiency has been linked to irritability, nervousness and an inability to relax; find calcium in dairy foods such as cheese, yoghurt and milk. Magnesium is often referred to as "nature's tranquilizer" and plays an essential role in helping the body absorb calcium; you can find it in dark green, leafy vegetables (such as broccoli, kale and spinach), seafood, potatoes, nuts, seeds and wholegrain products. A lack of zinc has been linked to depression; find zinc in seafood, eggs, broccoli, mushrooms, nuts, seeds and kiwis. Depleted iron levels in your diet can lead to low mood and anxiety, so it's important to ensure that you eat sufficient iron to maintain your levels of calm. Women need to keep an eye on their iron levels, as they tend to need more than men, and vegetarians might want to think about taking a supplement; find iron in dark-green, leafy vegetables, meat, fish, beans, pulses, nuts and wholegrain products.

Without accepting the fact that everything changes, we cannot find perfect composure.

Shinichi Suzuki

Try supplements

There are several herbal supplements that could help you feel calmer. Valerian, hops and passion flower have all been found to relieve stress, as well as promote healthy sleep; and while rhodiola rosea has been found to help with mild anxiety, it is also said to boost concentration. St John's Wort is used to treat mild to moderate depression and has been found to assist in balancing mood, but if you decide to try taking it, consult a doctor or pharmacist as it can react with several common prescription medicines, including the contraceptive pill.

STAY HYDRATED

Dehydration won't disturb your calmness on its own, but if you are already suffering from stress and tension, it may well aggravate your condition. If you are prone to panic attacks, it's especially important to stay hydrated as this will lessen the chances of you experiencing common symptoms, which could trigger an attack, such as headaches, feeling light-headed, muscle weakness and an increased heart rate. The European Food Safety Authority recommends 1.6 litres of fluid a day for women and 2 litres for men, so try to get used to carrying a bottle of water around with you, and take frequent drinks to stay hydrated. Don't forget that hot drinks, fruit juices and food also contain water, and so count towards your recommended daily intake.

EXERCISING YOUR WAY TO CALMNESS

During exercise, the body releases serotonin, the "happy hormone", which is both a mood booster and stress buster. Being more active will help you to relax in your downtime, sleep better and increase positivity, all of which will ultimately help make you calmer.

JUST WALK

Walking is such a simple form of exercise and it can be incorporated into your daily life with ease. Adding regular walking into your routine will help keep you fit and healthy, as well as having the added benefit of boosting feelings of tranquillity, due to the serotonin produced. There are a number of ways that you can introduce walking into a busy schedule, such as leaving earlier for work and parking further from the office, taking the dog for a walk before setting off in the morning, or going for a 20-minute stroll at lunchtime in a local park or by a river. It's a healthy habit to form and you'll soon be reaping the benefits, not just from the exercise but also by spending time out in the fresh air, which will have a calming effect on both body and mind.

He who lives in
harmony with himself
lives in harmony
with the world.

Marcus Aurelius

LET YOUR TROUBLES FLOAT AWAY

Swimming is one of the most effective forms of exercise, both in terms of giving you a full-body workout, which will leave you tired for all the right reasons, and in allowing you to relax and unwind. The rhythmic lap of the water with each stroke and the focus on your breathing make swimming a wonderfully calming activity. Use the first 20 minutes of your lunch hour for a swim, or take a stroll down to the seaside or open-air lido after work on a warm summer's afternoon, hop in the water and allow the day's stresses to float away.

Adopt the pace
of nature:
her secret is
patience.

Ralph Waldo
Emerson

GET ON YOUR BIKE

As well as being an efficient mode of transport, cycling is the perfect way to fit exercise into your daily routine. If you currently drive to work, or use public transport, and the distance is manageable, think about dusting off your steed and cycling to work instead. Fresh air and exercise are a good combination to help raise positivity levels, and regular cycling could go a long way to easing your mind while strengthening your body. If you'd rather take the scenic route, visit the Sustrans website, www.sustrans.org.uk, and learn about the cycling routes in your area. The UK National Cycle Network comprises 14,000 miles of safe, traffic-free paths and quiet road routes throughout the country, and Sustrans claims that a safe NCN route passes within a mile of 55 per cent of all UK homes. There's a wealth of green space on the outskirts of your home town just waiting to be explored, so get on your bike and ride your way to a more positive outlook.

LET
GO. OF
WHAT YOU
CAN'T
CONTROL.

GIVE YOGA A GO

Yoga can be practised in several different forms, but the ideal type to improve calmness is hatha. Hatha yoga is a gentle form of exercise that involves moving the body into, and holding, various postures, while maintaining slow, regular breathing. Designed to improve posture, strengthen muscles and increase flexibility, yoga also aims to help clear your mind and instil a sense of calm, and has been found to greatly help with alleviating stress and anxiety. You're likely to find several yoga options available locally, but start with something fairly gentle and meditative. If you can't find a hatha class or would rather try it out on your own first, buy one of the many DVDs available and practise in the comfort of your own home.

When we are
unable to find
tranquillity
within ourselves,
it is useless to seek
it elsewhere.

François de La Rochefoucauld

Relaxing

If your hectic lifestyle is making you feel frazzled, relaxation techniques can bring you back into balance. Experiment with the methods in this section and find the technique that works best for you.

Practise mindfulness

Mindfulness is a technique adopted from Buddhist teachings that can help you to live in the moment. This is a great way to cultivate peace of mind. Training your mind to notice how you are feeling about situations as they arise can help you to recognize your stress triggers which, in turn, makes it easier to be mindful of when they arise and to deal with them calmly. Mindfulness also helps us learn not to go into "autopilot' when we are doing familiar tasks, as this can be a cause of stress. Taking a shower with a mindful approach is a simple example: rather than just automatically going through the motions, notice how the water feels on your skin, the smell and texture of your body wash, the way your muscles relax with the heat. This can be a great way to start the day feeling unrushed and calm, and these techniques can be applied to your whole day.

Breathe

Sometimes we find it hard to switch off after a stressful day. A simple way to start training your body to relax is to practise mindful deep breathing. This can be done at any time of the day, whether before bed, first thing in the morning or at your desk in the office. The practice is simple: close your eyes and focus on your breath. Think only about your breath and the way it feels coming into your body and then out. Once you are fully aware of your breathing, try taking deeper breaths, breathing in for a count of six and then out for a count of six. Stay focused on your breath for five minutes. Integrating this exercise into your daily routine will help you on the way to feeling more relaxed.

A CLEAR mind IS THE KEY TO A SIMPLE LIFE.

YOUR MIND WILL ANSWER MOST QUESTIONS IF YOU LEARN TO RELAX AND WAIT FOR THE ANSWER.

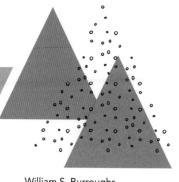

William S. Burroughs

Meditate

Meditation has been used by many cultures around the world for centuries. Yoga and t'ai chi are both described as "moving meditation", showing that this practice takes many forms. Put simply, meditation is a way of quieting your mind and allowing yourself time to be still. You don't necessarily have to sit cross-legged and chant mantras to meditate, though you can if this is something you find helpful. A good way to start, if meditation is new to you, is to sit in a comfortable position with a straight back, resting your hands palms-up in your lap. Close your eyes and focus on one of your other senses, such as your hearing. When your mind begins to wander, gently bring it back to your chosen sense. Doing this for five to ten minutes can make a huge difference to your day.

Make time for yourself

If you have other people in your life to worry about and you find this adds to your anxieties, then be sure to set aside time just for you. When there's a lot going on, it's important to have time to yourself to relax and gather your thoughts. Whether you spend an evening curled up with a good book or your favourite film or take yourself off for a scenic walk, find the time to do something you enjoy and appreciate your own company. Going for a run or a swim will give you a chance to think about your day, while doing something that will have a positive effect on your body and mind.

Everything you
do can be done

Better

from a place of

Relaxation.

Stephen C. Paul

Treatments and Therapies

When everything gets too much, complementary therapies can help to reduce the physical and mental symptoms of stress, and provide you with some much needed "me" time.

Seek cognitive
Behavioural Therapy

Cognitive behavioural therapy (CBT) is a form of psychotherapy that helps you to focus on replacing negative thoughts and behaviour with a more positive outlook. Your negative thoughts and behaviour affect your feelings, and this is what leads you to feel anxious. Cognitive theory claims our negative thoughts come from experiences throughout childhood and early adulthood, which often stay with us as we go through life. It works on the principles that you can change these perceptions of negativity by focusing on the present, with practical ways to improve your outlook on a daily basis, thus eventually altering the way you think and behave. The Mind website, www.mind.org.uk, is a good source of information and will help you to locate a therapist in your area.

Aromatherapy
for calm

Essential oils have long been used to help calm the mind and body. It is believed that inhaling the smells from essential oils affects the hypothalamus, the part of the brain that controls the glands and hormones, thereby changing a person's mood and lowering their stress levels. You can use aromatherapy oils in massage oil, in the bath, for steam inhalation or as a compress. Some uplifting essential oils to try include bergamot, chamomile, lavender, neroli and rose. Some stimulating oils to try include black pepper, geranium, peppermint and rosemary.

IT'S ALL
IN THE
REFLEXES

Reflexology, similarly to acupressure, uses
stimulation of certain points to help the
flow of energy through the body. These
points are found on the feet, hands and
face, but practitioners will usually use the
feet as these are more sensitive, and are
believed to have points that relate to every
part of the body. Stimulating these points
is meant to release energy blockages in
the related body part, therefore facilitating
the free flow of energy through that
body part, and reducing illness.

Whatever the health claims, the
relaxation alone will help you to feel
calmer. For practicality, if you decide
to try this on yourself, it may be
easier to use your hands, but, though
reflexology can be self-practised, it is
more relaxing to visit a reflexologist for
treatment. Look up your local natural
health centre for more information.

Be flexible

Everything is easier when you're open to change

EMBRACE ESSENTIAL OILS AND MASSAGE

Massage can help to relieve any physical tension you might be feeling and will have a soothing effect on your mind, too. You could opt for a professional massage or ask your partner to help. There is a range of essential oils that are thought to have a calming influence, so use one of these to enhance the benefits of the massage. Alternatively, you could dab a little on to your wrists or behind your ears, so the scent stays with you, and this may help you to relax throughout your day. Bergamot and jasmine are known for their calming and uplifting capabilities, while lemon balm and lavender are thought to help relieve stress and anxiety.

After all, the best thing
one can do when it's
raining is to let it rain.

Henry Wadsworth Longfellow

Believe that life is worth living and your belief will help create the fact.

William James

SMILE

AND THE WORLD WILL

SMILE BACK

AT YOU.

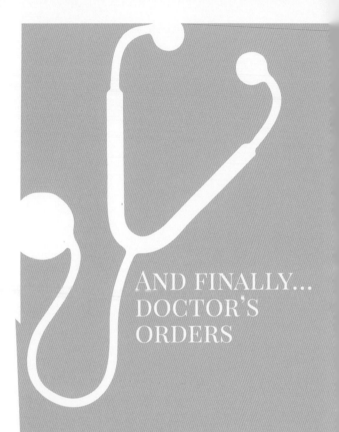

AND FINALLY...
DOCTOR'S
ORDERS

If you've given everything else a try and your worries are still proving too much for you, it could be time to seek professional help. Go to your GP first and see what they suggest – they may recommend seeing a therapist, someone you can talk to about your concerns; or cognitive behavioural therapy; or even medication. Remember to be honest with your doctor – try not to hold back, and give as much detail as possible – and they'll be able to suggest the right solution for you and your worries. Complementary therapies can help a great deal to reduce the stresses and strains that could be causing you to feel unbalanced but, sometimes, professional help is what's needed. You'll be on the right track and in safe hands, and will feel the benefit before you know it.

WE HOPE YOU ENJOY
THE JOURNEY TOWARDS
A NEW, CALMER YOU!

If you're interested in finding out more about our books,
find us on Facebook at Summersdale Publishers
and follow us on Twitter at @Summersdale.

WWW.SUMMERSDALE.COM